Contents

Chapter 1: Introduction

About this book

This book has been updated in 2022 and includes over 50% more content than the original published version. This update contains more information and insights on concepts around pricing, gamification and rewards, social proof and much more!

Want to know how to grow your sales easier or why people do - or do not buy from you? Then this book is for you.

In this book, we discuss how the customer's mind works and how you can be more effective in your sales and marketing by making some relatively small changes to the way you do things (and some bigger changes as well of course).

Quite often when we talk about modern marketing we think of social media, email marketing, and other channels, but these are just channels to reach out to our target audience.

Getting the customer to love your brand and make a purchase is a lot more complex and there is plenty of research that shows how, with just a few small changes to the way we do our marketing and selling, you can convert more potential customers into sales - and in less time.

In this book, we discuss various ways you can be more successful in your marketing by looking at various elements such as:

- The product design including its packaging
- Pricing of products and services
- Messages in advertising or any other communication with your customers
- The processes you use to attract and convert inquiries into customers

This is just a few of the items we will discuss in this book which, although being relatively short and concise, is crammed full of tips and advice.

The geek-free zone

If you are worried that we will flood your mind with complicated theories, tedious statistics and scientific terms, fear not!

This book does not go into an in-depth analysis of human psychology, but it does base the suggestions and principles on tested and proven research carried out by a large number of established sources.

I don't want to send you to sleep, so I have kept each chapter short and, in a bite-size format so that you can quickly understand what you can do with your sales and marketing - and why!

This book is also part of a mini-series of short books to help business owners, marketers and salespeople understand how to grow their business.

For further information on individual concepts, links to sources are provided, or you can visit the Think Twice Marketing blog page where there are lots of FREE articles exploring how to increase sales and be more effective in your marketing.

A big thanks for choosing this book Psychology in Marketing and Sales. I am sure that if you apply the principles in this book, you WILL generate more business and grow your sales. Enjoy!

A quick look at the figures

Many of the decisions you make on a daily basis could be losing you business.

This might sound like a bold claim, but understanding how customers behave when making decisions to engage with your brand or buy from you can help make better marketing and sales decisions.

Just applying small changes such as adding different wording on your website or making minor changes to the way you price your products could increase sales considerably. Let's take a quick example.

Imagine spending money on a marketing campaign that reaches a target audience of 2,000 people, and you know that you have a 1% conversion rate.

That's 20 customers out of a total audience of 2,000 people reached from the campaign.

By understanding what words or images make potential customers more likely to buy, you can increase sales.

Let's now imagine that the small changes you make lead to a conversion rate increase from 1% to 2%.

That still means that 98% of your audience see your campaign but don't buy from you, but the impact on sales and profit can be significant.

A new conversion rate of 2% is an extra 20 new customers which, at an average selling price of $100, is an extra $2,000 in sales!

Who could have imagined that just from making a few changes to the wording or images on your website that you can generate so much more business!

In the upcoming chapter in this book, we will go through the different concepts and ways that customers react to the way that you price, position or offer your products and services.

About The Author

Before we get started, here's a really quick overview of me (Darren Hignett). It won't take long, and it's a great way to set the scene for what you are about to read about. Here goes...

Not that I need a reminder of my age, but I have more than 25 years of experience working in marketing roles ranging from corporate businesses with marketing activities on a worldwide scale to running a business supporting small to medium businesses as well as start-ups.

While in the corporate world, I was heavily involved in marketing activities focused on how the consumers' mind works and what makes a customer decide to buy - or not.

This included finding the answers to questions such as:

- If you increase, decrease or bundle pricing, what happens?
- If you reduce the number of options for a potential customer, will that lead to more purchases?
- And does different wording or positioning a product differently affect the decision-making process?

Before the joys of corporate life and running my own business, I studied a marketing-focused degree in International Business - a 4-year course with a very strong focus on marketing theory.

This included concepts such as how to define your target market, how to understand their needs and how to create the right message and benefits in a way that customers understand and in a way that they will want to buy from you (bear in mind that the internet was only just coming of age at the time so a lot of marketing theory was based on areas such as features/benefits, having a marketing plan and how the customer thinks, rather than today's digital marketing).

This book shares my knowledge and experience as well as my many years of research and expertise in understanding how to use simple-to-apply tactics in sales and marketing to get proven business results.

Today, I provide coaching and mentoring to business owners to help them achieve better results in their sales and marketing.

I also run Think Twice Marketing, a digital marketing agency with the objective of helping businesses worldwide to be more effective in their sales and marketing.

But, enough of me. Let's get down to how you can generate more business using various strategies and tactics…

Chapter 2: Comparison and positioning

Whether we admit it or not, when it comes to buying or having things, we can't help but compare what we are looking at to different alternatives.

Sometimes, this can be a good thing as we check to make sure that what we are about to buy is the best offer, or the right product compared to alternative products out there.

Sometimes it can be a bad thing as we buy things and then immediately wish we had the next or higher-level product or, as the saying goes, we want to 'keep up with the Joneses'.

Whatever the reason for comparing products, pricing and what we have or are about to buy, it's something that sales and marketing people often don't take any enough notice of.

While potential customers are comparing various aspects relative to other offerings to make sure it's what they want, businesses can also use this to their advantage to steer the potential buyer in the right direction and to make the right choice.

In this chapter, we look at some simple concepts around how consumers compare things and what you can do to influence the decision process.

Anchoring

Anchoring is a technique that is often used on TV shopping channels. They start off talking about a product at a specific price (the anchor price) and then start presenting a special offer price that's lower.

Assume you come across a product you might want to buy but you are checking out the price and possibly want a bit more information about the product before buying.

If I tell you the price is $45 or £45, would you buy it?

You might. You might not. But what if I approached the pricing differently.

Imagine I haven't just told you the final price. Imagine I told you it's usually $120 or £120 but I'm reducing the price to $45 or £45.

Now, are you more or less likely to buy that product?

Put in context of this book, you might be influenced differently to actually being in the store or seeing the pricing online.

There might be other factors you consider, such as 'if the price is reduced, is something wrong with it - or is it the end of the product line – but, regardless of these factors, anchoring works.

During a presentation I was delivering to local businesses on the topic of pricing, I went through the concept of anchoring and one business owner pointed out that she had seen a branded pair of boots she really liked and was annoyed when a special offer ended, and the boots returned to their normal price.

Despite really wanting to buy them, she refused to make the purchase and waited until the next promotional campaign, when the boots were reduced again in price.

Even though there were plenty of good quality alternatives at the lower price, she had created the perception in her mind that the boots were worth more, and it was worth waiting for a special offer because she was getting a bargain.

I'm sure we all have examples like this where we have been enticed by an offer and perceived the offer to be a great bargain because the offer has been 'anchored' to a higher price.

Anchoring works because we set our expectations at the original price, and we feel like we are getting a reward or deal when the new price is presented.

The appeal becomes even greater when the price is dropped again and possibly again…

Anchoring doesn't just apply to when setting pricing. It can apply to the number of products you add to a bundle or the quality of a product.

If the first offer you present is improved upon by adding more products to a bundled offering, or by improving the quality with a new, updated product then a customer perceives a greater value in the new offer.

It goes something like this…

Today you can sign up to buy this amazing software for £195 or $195 but I'm going to exceed your expectations.

I'm including access to a private Facebook Group with top tips and tricks to help you.
I will also include an eBook on how to perform what you want to do even better (worth $30)
I will also include a scheduled 60-minute video call to run through how to use the software
AND instead of the normal 30-day money-back guarantee, I will increase it to a huge 90 days!

Are you convinced?

You might not like all of the extras listed here, but at the back of your mind, you are subconsciously adding up all of these extras that aren't 'normally' included and telling yourself it's a bargain.

If they were always included as part of the package, you might not be quite as convinced to buy.

Anchoring can also be used in setting expectations, and the follow-on offer must always be better.

If you promise a 5-day delivery and deliver it in 3 days, then the customer is delighted.

If, however, you promise delivery in 2 days, then the customer will be disappointed when it's delivered in 3 days, despite the fact that it's the same delivery timeframe as the first example.

Anchoring works because it's a way to compare two or more elements in an offer. This is discussed further in the section below on relativity.

Marketing Relativity, Not Einstein's

You've heard of Einstein's law of relativity, but marketing relativity is a different concept - and a much easier concept to understand!

Imagine you are considering a short break to either Rome or Paris. You compare the options relative to each other.

The quotes you receive are identical - the same number of nights in the city, in a similar hotel, same flight options, etc. Which one do you go for?

Paris - 4 nights - $800
Rome - 4 nights - $800

In a survey discussed by Dan Ariely in his book 'Predictably Irrational', around half of the people who were asked selected Paris, and half selected Rome. But when a third and undesirable option was added the results changed considerably.

By adding a second Paris option that was exactly the same again but with breakfast not included, the majority of people in the survey went for the original option to go to Paris.

Paris - 4 nights - $800
Paris - 4 nights - $800 (breakfast not included)
Rome - 4 nights - $800

Why?

It turns out that when we are given just two options that are identical, we compare these two options, but by adding a third option that is for Paris, the mind stops comparing Rome and instead compares the two Paris options.

We then notice how the first option to go to Paris is a better option, compared to the second option and we go with that.

In many circumstances, we ignore the Rome package completely.

Launching inferior products to grow sales...?

The idea of launching inferior products to grow sales might sound bizarre, and it's not something I endorse - but there's a great example of this which we can learn from!

When Williams-Sonoma first launched their bread maker for $275, sales were poor.

Despite their marketing efforts, consumers didn't get the concept of making bread at home - and why they should pay $275 for such a device.

More thought into improving the product, it seemed, was needed. Make the product better and sales will come, right? So, what did Sonoma do?

They launched a larger, heavier and less attractive bread maker at a 50% price premium.

You might want to read that again - they launched a product that was effectively less attractive.

Although it had a few more features, it was larger and carried a 50% premium over the original product that was still available to buy.

What happened was unexpected. Sales of Williams-Sonoma bread makers started to really take off - but not for the new premium-priced product, it was for the original machine priced at $275.

Why had this happened?

The answer, it seems, is relativity.

On its own, the $275 bread maker had nothing to compare against. Possibly a coffee maker instead of a bread maker (which was much cheaper) or some other kitchen appliance? Or maybe the idea of keeping $275 in your pocket?

Once the new bread maker was launched, consumers were saying "wow, this original bread maker is much better value for money and is smaller than the new one, I think I'll take that one" rather than "a bread maker? Not sure why I want to pay over $200 for that!".

The conversation in their mind had shifted from whether to buy at all to which one should I buy.

How can you use this in your business?

If you are in the travel and tourism business, then the above is a great example of how you can make trips to Paris more attractive. Here are some more examples for other businesses:

A printing business can promote its higher quality business card packages, by offering different options to the customer for the higher quality print packages, but then only offer one option for the lower priced budget package.

A sports coach can promote a sport or session by offering more options for that sport than other types of sports.

A food retailer can promote a premium brand by offering a mid-range product at a very similar price using what's known as decoy pricing, making the premium brand much more attractive.

Action!

How can you use anchor pricing and relativity in your marketing to generate more sales? I recommend putting 20 minutes aside now to consider the following:

-Can/should I change how my prices are displayed to show a reduce price (anchoring)
-Can/should I also change how prices are shown side by side (relativity)
-Do I need to launch a new product or service to give customer's s something to compare?
-Alternatively, could a new product increase sales by being superior to what you currently have?
-Can you run a sales and marketing campaign that uses anchoring and relativity to grow sales?

There's plenty more to think about when discussing marketing campaigns, pricing and what products or services you offer, and we will be covering those in upcoming chapters.

Pricing and perception are very closely aligned, and we will discuss the theory of concept called decoy pricing later in the chapter on pricing.

Chapter 3: Fear and the senses

In this chapter, we will talk about how fear at various levels can impact the decision-making process.

The focus here is not on scaring customers or being unethical in any way. It's about harnessing the various fears we have, no matter how small, and helping potential customers to overcome those fears with the solutions that you have.

We will also talk about how smell and sounds impact the decisions consumers make and how, by using the right smells and sounds, you can make what you offer more attractive.

Scarcity and the power of fear

Do you suffer from FOMO?

The term FOMO (or fear of missing out) has actually been around a long time but has become a lot more popular in the last 5-10 years.

Whatever the history of the term FOMO, humans have worried or acted on the fear of not having something for a long time - and not just the fear of missing out on what our friends are up to!

As hunter-gatherers, not knowing when the next meal will be available and how many days we would have to go without food meant that we had to take what's available to us now without wasting time.

Scarcity of resources has taught us to act on impulse before it's too late, and this has been used in many ways over the years.

Remember the flight reservation you made when the website said, "only 2 seats left"? Or the offer you took up online when it had the message "offer ends in 2 hours"?

Scarcity can include the amount of time before an offer ends, or a limited number of stock on products that you are selling.

Used ethically, the scarcity factor can be a very powerful marketing tool.

I say 'ethically' as it's important to provide accurate information to the customer. If you say there are only 5 products left, but you actually have a warehouse full, then this is misleading for the customer and not something I endorse.

Scarcity is best used when running a promotion, and the less there is available of time (before the promotion ends) or stock, then the more likely the promotion will be a success. Assuming of course, that you have communicated this in your marketing!

Over the years, I have found that special offers run over a longer period are less successful than offers that end very soon. Take these two examples:

A - Save 40%. Offer ends in 2 weeks
B - Save 40%. Offer ends in 2 hours

During a busy day, we might see offer A and say to ourselves, 'I'll come back to that later', and we most likely won't.

We will forget or lose the email or URL where we came across the offer, leading to a lost sale for the business promoting the offer.

If, however, we see offer B, and we know we are about to miss out then we instinctively take action to buy what's on offer. We might not really want what's on offer, but we end up buying it anyway because we don't want to miss out!

If you are running a marketing campaign for a limited time offer, make sure to keep promoting the offer by providing a countdown.

On social media, you might post the launch of the offer, saying it finishes in 2 days followed by another post saying there are less than 24 hours, then less than 6 hours, and then less than 2 hours left.

The frequency of reminders depends on what the offer is, how long it's running for and what channels you are using.

Campaigns can run for longer, especially if there is a lot of work managing the campaign, or if it's a larger scale purchase - but always bear in mind that most of the sales are likely to take place as the offer comes to an end.

The power of fear

When it comes to making a purchase, understanding the benefits of a product or service helps us to decide if it's something we want to buy, but there are two ways to position those benefits - in a positive light, such as 'enjoy the experience of...' and in the way of fear, for example, 'avoid having to lose out on…'.

Whilst it's good to include a mix of both types of benefits, the human mind responds better to fear of loss, or suffering.

According to Inc.com[1] '*Fear is a universal condition, one that leaves most of us searching for ways to get back to our comfort zones.*'

Hubspot[2] expands on this further saying '*We're chemically wired to react to fear at a primal level. Whether someone's putting a knife to our neck or you're falling short on your sales numbers this quarter, your brain will start pumping chemicals throughout your body to create a fight-or-flight response.*'

When we talk about promoting a product based on fear, we aren't talking about scaring people out of their wits or painting a doomsday or apocalypse scenario.

---

[1] Read the full article at https://www.inc.com/heather-r-morgan/how-to-effectively-sell-through-fear-without-going-too-far.html

[2] See: https://blog.hubspot.com/sales/use-fear-to-sell

We are simply finding the pain points a customer has and highlighting what the consumer might be missing out on, or how life might not be so good without having what you offer.

Using fear wrongly can have a negative impact.

Selling based on fear is used more widely than you might think, from the shortage of seats left when booking a flight (only 2 seats left, don't miss out!) to pensions, investments and car breakdown cover (don't get stranded on your own with your car broken down…) to the range of every day offers you see, telling you that if you don't take advantage of the offer in the next 24 hours, then you will miss out.

Here are some examples of effective positive and fear-based messages for different types of businesses.

How do you feel when you read the two versions? Do the different statements impact the way you feel differently?

Enjoy a happy retirement by investing in a pension now
Don't lose out on a happy retirement with limited money to live on, invest in a pension now

Protect your PC from viruses with antivirus software
Avoid losing data and precious time recovering your PC with antivirus software

Beat the queues with fast pass
Make sure you don't waste hours queuing up. Grab your fast pass now

Stay safe with our new style bike helmet

Protect yourself from serious injury with our new style bike helmet

Fear based selling should also be subtle, as you may have noticed in a few of the above examples.

To avoid being too negative, it's recommended to use some positive (none fear based) benefits as well.

The next time you work on your marketing, consider how you can develop your messaging and the benefits by pointing out both what's great about what you offer AND what your potential customers could be missing out on.

Using smell and sounds

According to QZ.com[3]* smell can impact what we buy, 'People will feel more comfortable, and they'll pay more for products that smell the way we imagine them to smell.' but does this just apply to perfume and flowers?

Evidence shows that this applies to a whole range of products from cars (with that new car smell) to sofas, restaurant food, and coffee at your local coffee shop.

In season 4 (Episode 7) of Brain Games hosted by National Geographic, they perform an experiment trying to sell roadkill food from a food truck on the side of the road.

---

[3] Read the full article at https://qz.com/1349712/companies-like-starbucks-use-smells-to-keep-us-buying-heres-why-it-works/

After not getting any interest from people passing by in their options including 'blackened beavertail' or 'iguana lasagna' they added the sounds of sizzling meat and the smell of wafting bacon - and the results?

Not just a few people stopped to find out what was available - queues actually started to form with growing numbers wanting to buy their lunch from the food truck.

One person after purchasing, actually asked if they could have more food to go!

By adding the sounds and smells that we are familiar with, people passing by couldn't resist what was earlier dismissed as undesirable, disgusting or even strange.

Who wants to eat roadkill food with a slogan saying 'you kill it we eat it'? Apparently, many of us once the right sounds and smells are applied.

Whether you own a retail store, cafe, restaurant or any other location where customers can make purchases, make sure that you are considering what the surroundings - and in particular the smell is like.

Stinky and stale might not get the sale, but the right smell could make all the difference!

Chapter 4: Pricing

I am always surprised by how little information, or credible advice there is on pricing products.

When it comes to social media, email marketing, closing down a sale or one of many other topics around marketing and sales, there is always plenty of top tips and advice from experts - but when it comes to pricing? There's very little information to be found.

Ever since my days working in corporate, I have been researching the best and most effective ways to price products and services and on many occasions, I've been involved in some lively debates over questions such as, 'what happens if we increase pricing by x%' or, 'should the promotion offer include an add-on for FREE, or for a nominal $1'?

These might sound like trivial 'who cares?' type of debates, but the impact on a marketing campaign or the very success of a product can be huge.

Badly priced products can lead to misconceptions over the quality or functionality of a product, yet we often focus on the other elements of sales and marketing without really thinking through prices.

I have seen Product Managers in corporate businesses spend months designing products and working with engineers to create the 'perfect solution', only to quickly stick a price tag on it at the last minute that's in line with competitor pricing, and calculated based on what the estimated costs are, plus a standard percentage margin, of say, 40%.

Why is this a bad thing?

Other than the fact that it's not properly thought through, and could be losing sales, one major opportunity that's missed is what the value is to the customer.

Just because you have a cost price of x, and the margin should be a set percentage, doesn't mean that it's the best price you can charge your customer.

Imagine you have a cost price of $100 and decide to sell it at $160. That sounds good, but what if I told you that the product can save a customer thousands of dollars over its lifetime?

What if the customer valued the product at $500, $600 or even over a thousand dollars, and they would be prepared to pay that, because it's worth it?

Assuming you only sell 100 units over a year, then underpricing by $400 means $40,000 a year in missed revenue!

Selling based on value is just one example of how businesses are missing out on substantial business growth.

In the rest of this chapter, we will also look at ways to position pricing options, as well as how FREE can actually increase sales and profits.

Yes, you read that right, after talking about higher prices, I'm going to convince you that some solutions could make you more money by giving them away!

Decoy Pricing

Decoy pricing is a very clever way to make a different product offering more attractive, by offering an inferior, or decoy price.

It's very similar to the concept of relativity (mentioned in a previous chapter) but the focus with decoy pricing is on how a product or service is priced.

The term 'decoy pricing' was widely written about by Dan Ariely after he discovered it being used by the Economist magazine. He consequently undertook research to understand how decoy pricing worked.

Here's an example of Decoy Pricing being used:

A - Online content: $65
B - Printed learning materials: $130
C - Online access and printed learning materials: $130

In this example, the printed learning materials (option B) is the decoy price.

As it's the same price as the last option, but isn't as good value for money, then it doesn't make any sense to purchase this option and very few, if at all anyone, will go for option B - and the business offering these 3 options knows that.

If only options A and C are offered, then a buyer will compare option C with a lower-priced option A, and the majority of buyers will select option A.

When option B is introduced, however, more people purchase option C.

Here are the results from Dan Ariely's research:

With just two options:

A - Online content: $65. **68% purchased option A**
C - Online access and printed learning materials: $130. **32% purchased option C**

With the decoy pricing:

A - Online content: $65 **16% purchased option A**
B - Printed learning materials: $130
C - Online access and printed learning materials: $130 **84% purchased option C**

Just by introducing option B as the decoy pricing, the number of people who bought the premium service rose from 32% to 84%!

That's a considerable shift towards the higher-priced option, just by introducing decoy pricing.

The decoy option has focused the mind away from the lower-priced option and onto a comparison of the decoy pricing against the higher-priced option.

If you're offering package options to your customers, consider how decoy pricing could be used to grow your sales, and your profit margin!

Sale time! Percentage Vs. Pounds

You are having a sale to bring in some short-term sales, but do you promote how much money a customer could save, or do you focus on the percentage saving?

In other words, do you go with 'Save $5' or 'Save 50%'?

The answer to this comes down to a trade-off. It depends on the value, or the amount in Pounds, Dollars or Euros that are being saved versus how high the percentage saving is.

If you are promoting a relatively low-cost item, then mentioning a percentage saving will attract more sales.

The value in money doesn't sound so impressive, but the percentage saving does. For example, which one sounds like a better saving to you for a product that's normally $5?

A - Save $1
B - Save 20%

A dollar doesn't sound like much, but 20% is a lot more attractive.

If, however the value of the item is much more - say $1,000 - then promoting the actual amount of money that can be saved will make more sense. Which option now looks more appealing in this example?

A - Save $200
B - Save 20%

Now 20% doesn't sound so good, and the fact that $200 can be saved is a lot more appealing.

What about high percentage AND high value?

The results in these circumstances vary, and there are probably very few circumstances where you would do this.

Offering 80% off a $1,000 item means you are really selling at a rock bottom price, and as a general rule, it's best to go with the amount of money rather than the percentage that can be saved.

A customer might still say no to 80% off, but saving $800? Who would want to miss out on that?

Wording and other ways to promote a sale

When promoting based on value savings rather than as a percentage, it's worth showing the original price, so that the customer can see how much the price has dropped by (see the chapter on Anchoring for more information as well).

We have talked about using percentages or value, but there are other ways to promote a sale.

Straight forward discounting can impact the brand negatively, as people think there is something wrong with the product, it's the end of the product life or it's inferior to your competitors' products.

Another alternative is to offer extras for free. This way the product is not seen as being discounted.

The power of FREE is discussed later, but here are some alternatives to consider:

Instead of discounting a mobile phone or electrical device by $20, offer a free case.

The case might be worth $20 to the customer, but it will most likely cost you a lot less to buy!

Instead of offering 10 (or 11) fitness coaching sessions at 10% off, provide the 11th session completely FREE.

A 10% discount for committing to 10 sessions doesn't sound that great, but a full session completely FREE sounds like a great offer.

In this case, you have to deliver 11 sessions instead of 10 but at the full price.

Why FREE can bring in more sales

In his book, *Predictably Irrational*, Dan Ariely demonstrates how consumers are enticed so heavily by something free that it leads to decisions that might be worse off for them!

The 0% interest on a credit card for the first 3 months, followed by a much higher rate over the long term might be a worse decision for a consumer, compared to an option from another bank offering a lower rate with no special introductory offer, but the idea of 0 or interest being 'free' gets the sale.

Which one would you take?

A - Special Offer! 0% APR for 3 months! (19% APR after)
B - Standard rate 12% APR

I should point out that I'm not endorsing the idea of luring customers to make purchases that makes them worse off, or that you should start giving away your core products for free (after all the purpose of a business is to make money!) but using FREE as a marketing tool can be a highly effective way to succeed, to attract customers and start building a potentially long-term relationship with them.

So, why does FREE work?

According to Seth Godin in his marketing workshop[4], a customer's heart rate increases just before making their first purchase from a business.

This reflects the risks involved for the customer - the fact they are parting with money and the risks of buying from an unknown or unproven source.

---

[4] Available on Skillshare

There are other risks such as the item being faulty or a scammer taking credit card details and using them to steal money from you.

Buying a product may only be a small risk, such as parting with a few pounds or dollars, but the risk is enough to put a potential customer off purchasing.

According to Seth, offering an item for free removes those risks, and stops or lowers the consequent increase in heart rate.

If the first 'purchase' is free, such as a trial or free consultation providing advice, then you are more likely to build trust with the customer. They are then more likely to make what would be classed as a second purchase involving spending money.

Here are some examples of how FREE can be used in your marketing to attract customers to take the first step:

Classes: Attend the first class for FREE
Gym: FREE 7-day trial
Software: FREE basic version or 14-day trial
Business/Career coach: FREE initial consultation
Drinks business: FREE cup, mug or wine glass with every purchase
Car mechanic: FREE car clean with every full service
Tourist attraction: Kids go FREE
Mobile phone: FREE carry case with every 2-year contract

When offering extras for free, it's important to make sure that you aren't giving away money that you could otherwise be earning by selling those items.

The extra item should also be something that doesn't cost you much, but which might be of high value to the client.

In the mobile phone example, the carry case might cost you only a few dollars, but it has a much higher value to the customer.

Do a check to see how much the item costs you in time and money, and also how many extra sales you will attract on your main product, compared to the sales of the extra item.

For example, a car mechanic might be selling only a few car cleans every week, but by offering a free car clean with every service then they might sell 5 or more car services a day!

The extra sales from car servicing far outweigh any lost sales for car cleaning.

Added to this, a customer might decide to use their car cleaning services again in the future after experiencing how great a job has been done.

Price and design can impact the experience

You've probably heard the saying 'you get what you pay for', but when it comes to wines and other food and drinks that can be found in a supermarket, you might also have wondered if the premium branded products are really 3 or 4 times better, as the price suggests.

In many situations, paying a higher price reflects better quality, but there is a second element to this. Having a higher price can actually convince us that a product looks, feels or tastes better, when in fact it isn't necessarily better!

The design of the packaging - such as the shape and label of a wine bottle, or appearance of a mobile phone, can also influence our belief about if a product is better or not.

There have been various studies showing how the price or appearance of a product can influence our experience.

In 2 experiments by Dan Ariely[5], participants were tested to see how much pain they felt during tests.

In the first test, participants were given a branded placebo pain killer which was proven to reduce the pain. They didn't know the pain killer was a placebo, but the participants felt pain relief, even though it was simply a capsule containing Vitamin C.

In a second follow on experiment, participants were tested to see how price impacted the results. Here's what they found:

"In our next test, we changed the brochure, scratching out the original price ($2.50 per pill) and inserting a new discount price of 10 cents. Did this change our participants' reaction? Indeed. At $2.50 almost all our participants experienced pain relief from the pill. But when the price was dropped to 10 cents, only half of them did."

-Dan Ariely, Predictably Irrational

Note, I'm not suggesting that medication doesn't work at all - or that we can all feel better and cure ourselves simply by using placebos or thinking positive.

---

[5] In his book Predictably Irrational, chapter 'The power of price'.

The point here is that perception in any product or service plays a big part in how we feel about what is being offered.

In other tests, participants have regarded wine to taste better based on the bottle it's poured from, and the style and name on the label of the bottle - even when the contents are swapped around so that the cheaper wine is served from the premium branded bottle!

The key takeaway here is that how you price your offerings and design the appearance of it, including its packaging, will impact how potential customers perceive or feel about it.

If you have a quality product but price it too low, for example, then it's more likely to be regarded as not so good, even after being used by customers!

Similarly, a consumers' brain can trick itself to believe that a product is much better (even if it isn't) if the design and appearance is right. More on that later…

Chapter 5: Design & Rewards

In his chapter, we will discover how different product designs can impact the way a customer thinks when buying a product, as well as how they use what they have purchased.

Great design can make a huge difference to how appealing a product is to a customer, and to how likely they are to make a purchase.

Although this section focuses a lot on physical products that are tangible, and which customers can see and touch, it can also refer to services.

A business selling memberships such as for business networking or some form of ongoing support can increase the appeal of what they offer by giving out introductory materials or 'getting started' booklets, personal invites or even a free gift that's not tacky or poor quality.

These little extras can make the whole experience much nicer, and much more appealing, so long as the materials are designed correctly. Badly designed materials, however, can have a negative impact.

Great design also impacts customer loyalty. If a customer loves the product, then they are more likely to buy more, or come back to you when a product comes to the end of its natural life. Apple is a great example of this.

Many loyal customers love the design of their iPhones - not just of the shape and size of their mobile phones, but also how they feel when using the phone. In other words, the overall experience including the software, operating system and physical product itself is important.

Later on in the chapter, we will also briefly talk about using rewards, including gamification, in the design of what you offer.

Rewarding your customers is a great way to build long-term loyalty and we will go through how and why concepts such as gamification work, and how you can use it in your product design and marketing.

In this section we will now look at examples of how design impacts consumers at IKEA, with cars and even when buying ice cream, starting with IKEA...

The IKEA effect

Research shows that customers who are involved in a process (such as making or assembling their own furniture or being part of a discussion group) form a closer association with the brand.

This effect has been named the IKEA effect after research showed how people who bought IKEA or similar self-assembly furniture looked after their furniture better and kept it for longer than those who purchased furniture that was delivered fully assembled.

It's worth re-phrasing that and reflecting on it... customers who are involved in the process of making or manufacturing a product, form a closer bond or affiliation with the brand!

Wikipedia[6] explains:

"The IKEA effect was identified and named by Michael I. Norton of Harvard Business School, Daniel Mochon of Yale, and Dan Ariely of Duke, who published the results of three studies in 2011. They described the IKEA effect as "labor alone can be sufficient to induce greater liking for the fruits of one's labor: even constructing a standardized bureau, an arduous, solitary task, can lead people to overvalue their (often poorly constructed) creations."

If you want people to buy into your brand, and you want to build customer loyalty, then getting them involved in the solutions you offer is a great way to do this.

Asking them to complete surveys for future product development, as well as asking them to join Facebook community groups may not be quite as effective, but they are easy to implement activities that can make a difference in making customers and potential customers become true advocates of your brand.

The IKEA effect can be used in a number of other ways. Here are some examples:

If you offer a subscription delivery service, why not get customers to vote on, or decide what varieties or products should be in future deliveries!

Outlets selling food can offer the chance for customers to add ingredients such as toppings, and select what packaging they would like to take their purchase away in.

---

[6] source: https://en.wikipedia.org/wiki/IKEA_effect

Cars and ice cream

There's a lot to think about when buying a car, from what you can afford, whether you have a family and need to cater for them, and which brand you trust to how you plan to use the car (is it to get to work on the Interstate or Motorway or is it to run around town or the city?).

One aspect that many people will admit to being a factor, even if they reject the idea that it's very important, is the looks of the car on the outside.

Note: I have not said the inside or both the inside and outside! Just the outside.

In a showroom, there will have been many people over the years who have said, "That car looks nice", and then they gone on to check out the inside as well as other specs in more detail - while the 'not so nice' cars that might offer greater value or specs are passed over, without being checked out.

The crazy thing with this is that we spend most - if not ALL - of our time inside the car, and while we don't really spend our time staring at the inside of the cockpit while driving, it's still the area that's visible to us most of the time, and that we look at the most.

If you are one of those people who sits in the evenings, looking out of your lounge window admiring your car - my apologies, but you are definitely the exception!

Car manufacturers understand this. The outside design of a car is a great way to initiate interest, and prompt potential car buyers to find out more.

It is also, however, whether we admit it or not, a major factor in our decision making.

Sure - the entertainment system might not be to your liking or seats might not be comfy, and these are all factors in making the decision, but it's when you get out of the car in the showroom and step back, that you look at the car and say "I'd like to buy that one".

When designing your product, it's always important to think about the functionality and how easy the process is for using what you offer - but also consider how important the design or appearance is of things that might not even be used!

You might design the most effective microwave or toaster, but it's the great-looking ones that generate more interest if the consumer believes it will look great in their kitchen.

You might offer amazing perfumes, lotions, or skincare products but if the packaging and the bottles don't inspire consumers, then they may not get to find out how great your products really are.

I am not saying focus on exterior design at the cost of a great, or amazing product. The focus should always be on creating great products (unless you are in the me-too market of copying competitors and then undercutting them on price).

There have been many products over time that can be considered great products, but they failed to sell because they either looked ugly or were ahead of their time in looks and design, and consumers aren't prepared to buy a boring, unattractive looking product - no matter how well it performs the task it was designed to do.

I scream for ice cream

Even before the well-known song '*I Scream, You Scream, We All Scream for Ice Cream*' first came out in 1927, we have all loved ice cream and, since this delicious product with its many varieties is well known and so popular, there's no need to worry about packing design to attract customers, right? Wrong…

Research has shown that ice cream in round tubs is much more likely to be purchased than square tubs, despite the fact that their shape can be an inconvenience when storing them, and you typically get less ice cream (sorry to break that bad news if you weren't aware!).

The reason why round tubs are more attractive is because they look nicer and are considered to be more 'personal'.

It doesn't matter what variety or flavor of ice cream it is - round tubs sell more.

How are you designing your product?

It seems that it doesn't matter whether it's cars, ice cream, living room furniture, or something else, design and appearance is an important factor in whether a consumer buys your product.

Even if the appearance has no effect on the overall functionality of what you offer, it's worth spending time creating a great looking product.

Rewards

Rewards is also something that be part of the overall design when it comes create a solution or the customer experience.

Providing rewards to customers can take many forms ranging from loyalty card points that can be redeemed to simply rewarding a customer with extra support and materials after using your services for a while.

While loyalty marketing has been around for a number of years, gamification has become an interesting topic in marketing in recent years.

If you provide an online course, then you can reward students by providing them with points every time they reach a certain level of progress.

In many cases, the student doesn't need to receive any tangible reward. Instead, they become motivated by receiving points and seeing how high a score they can get.

Rewards can also take the form of having a league table. If you provide teambuilding events or group fitness training, then you can pitch customers (in a nice way) against each other to see who achieves the best results.

A small league table and a little bit of competition can be a great way to motivate attendees while making the product or service much more enjoyable.

If you aren't sure about how effective it is to use rewards, consider these facts:

Acquiring a new customer can be 5 to 25 times more expensive than keeping a customer through loyalty marketing.[7]

Customers who are engaged in a loyalty program or some form of gamification tend to spend more money over their lifetime as a customer.

The following companies have used gamification and loyalty marketing successfully[8]:

Texas bank Extracto created a gamified process to teach clients about what it offers and the benefits.
This led to a rise in conversion rates from 2% to 14%.
It also raised customer acquisition by 700%.

KFC Japan created gaming content that led to a 106% increase in store sales.

After launching the Starbucks Rewards app, Starbucks posted a revenue increase of $2.65 billion while its membership program increased by 25%

---

[7] https://www.annexcloud.com/blog/10-statistics-prove-effectiveness-loyalty-programs/

[8] https://financesonline.com/gamification-statistics/#:~:text=The%20gamification%20market%20size%20in, 2025%20(MarketsandMarkets%2C%202020)

Kenco increased its bottom-line sales margin by 45% after implementing a sales gamification tool for its customers.

How can you implement rewards in your business?

There are 3 main objectives of using reward-based marketing (whether that's loyalty marketing or some form of gamification):

1. Acquire more customers
2. Customer retention
3. Increase spend per customer

If you run a services-based business such as a café, restaurant or a subscription delivery business then consider using a loyalty program that rewards the customer after a certain number of purchases.

The classic example to consider is the café that provides a stamp or tick on their loyalty card every time they buy a tea or coffee.

They are then rewards with a free beverage when they have 10 stamps.

If you offer online courses or anything thing that requires achieving certain levels (include a gaming app – of course) then consider gamification and set points for various levels to encourage users to stay engaged and advance.

If you provide any services that's based on a group of people then you might also want to consider a league table with rewards for who comes top, and possibly anyone who has put in the most effort.

Here are a couple quick tips for implementing reward marketing:

Kick-start the program: Research shows that if you give users free points or stamps to get started then they are more motivated to take part and stay focused.

In one bit of research[9], 34% of users who were given 2 out of 10 slots already stamped for a car wash loyalty program filled their loyalty card, versus only 19% of those who were given a blank loyalty card.

According to Stampme.com:

"Known as the "endowed progress effect", researchers Joseph C. Nunes and Xavier Dreze tested the idea that if you provide some artificial advancement toward a goal, a person is more likely to complete the goal."

Vary the rewards: Casinos and email inboxes are classic examples of unpredictable rewards that keep us hooked.

If a customer doesn't know where and when they will get the reward, they become more determined to seek that reward.

In a casino, the reward from a slot machine is highly unpredictable and this sense of anticipation keeps us coming back for more.

---

[9] https://www.stampme.com/blog/accelerate-your-loyalty-program-give-your-customers-a-head-start

Bizarrely this also works with social media feeds and emails as we check them both constantly looking for the next bit of good news… but I digress!

According to Salesandmarketing.com:

"*The element of surprise has been proven to be a powerful motivational tool. Scientific studies show that unexpected incentive rewards stimulate areas of the brain connected to behavior development and learning.*"

There are various ways that you can make the rewards unpredictable and the best way, and levels that you set them at will depend on your product or service.

An eCommerce business might reward customers with an occasional boost in their reward points.

If a customer usually receives 1 point for every dollar or pound that they spend, you could randomly (or from time to time) provide them with an extra 20 or 30 points extra to thank them for being a customer.

Similarly, deliveries could sometimes arrive with an extra coupon or small gift to make the customer feel special.

Let's now discuss the importance of building trust with potential new customers, and how to do it…

Chapter 6: Building Trust

Would you buy from someone you don't trust?

With so many snake-oil salesmen and scams, we have learned over time to buy only from people and brands that we trust.

We might still fall for these tricks from time to time, but they are definitely the kind of businesses you want to stay away from – and they are the kind of business you don't want to run!

If you want to grow your business on a good reputation, and with happy delighted customers, then it's important to build trust with potential new buyers.

In fact, trust is incredibly important and highly undervalued.

When it comes to marketing, many businesses are often disappointed with email campaigns, telemarketing, advertising and other campaigns without realizing that the reason their campaign failed was due to a lack of trust.

I don't mean that their campaign was dodgy, or that they were promising something that looked overly exaggerated.

The lack of trust, I'm referring to is simply that the potential customer doesn't know the brand or the person selling well enough to want to buy from them.

You might call this familiarity – "sorry I don't know who you are, so I'd rather not buy from you", but it's very much about knowing enough about the business, the seller and/or the brand to trust them.

A business might send out an email campaign to a thousand recipients from an email list that they bought from a third-party.

Those thousand recipients have either never heard of the brand or know very little at all about them.

Sending a single email to someone who doesn't know the brand has got a very low chance of being a success, even with the best content copy in the world.

Whether it's networking, social media, telemarketing, email marketing or something else, trust needs to be built up -and we will go through this in more detail later on.

There are many elements to trust, including what reviews a brand has, who recommends them and how they talk to you and treat you during the sales process.

In this chapter, we focus on how you can get customers to become more familiar with you and trust you so that they are happy to use your services rather than your competitors... we will also briefly talk about not creeping them out during the trust building phase!

Building trust with the number 7

Seven seems to be a magic number. You've heard of the 7 wonders of the world, there are 7 days in a week, 7 notes on a musical scale, 7 colors in a rainbow, and if that isn't enough, Snow White met 7 dwarves while even the legendary British agent James Bond is 007. But what about marketing?

When it comes to building trust with potential customers, very few people will buy from an unknown brand, or from someone they don't know straight away.

Research has shown that the majority of purchases come after 5-7 contact points with a brand. In other words, a consumer will come into contact (known as touchpoints) on average 5-7 times before making their first purchase.

These touchpoints can include a phone call, receiving an email, interacting on social media or any other way in which you or your brand can reach out and interact with the potential buyer.

Don't give up!

You might think this is great to know, but so what? Consider these two statistics…

80% of purchases are made after 5-12 contact points

48% of salespeople never follow up after the FIRST touchpoint

And only 10% of salespeople will make more than 3 'contacts'[10].

---

[10] Information from
https://jmjdirect.wordpress.com/2010/01/14/how-many-contacts-does-is-take-to-make-a-sale-follow-up-is-the-key/

You might be running an online business without employing salespeople, but whatever your business, it's clear that a lot of customers require multiple contact points before they buy, and most businesses don't follow up anywhere near enough to get the sale.

I mention 7 contact points, but the actual number will vary depending on the individual, the business or industry you are in, and the type of contact points.

Doing a Google search on this topic, I came across articles and research with figures ranging from '6-8 touchpoints' to '8-9 touchpoints' and even one article saying '5 to 12 touchpoints'.

While different research reveals slightly different results, the key point is that very few people buy after just one or two touchpoints, and most purchases come within the 5-7 range.

Some articles also disputed what a touchpoint was. Does Liking a post on Facebook count, for example, or is it not enough of an interaction?

Whilst many people often Like posts without fully reading the content of the post, I would still count it.

Liking a post means that a customer has seen your post (including your avatar which should be your brand logo), they have at least stopped scrolling to focus in on your brand, and to make a positive action to Like your post.

Although this data is quite old, similar more recent articles quote similar figures.

Having a two-way chat over the phone, or face to face, might be much more impactful and meaningful for the potential buyer, but interacting through various channels should be considered including:

Emails
Phone Calls
Social Media Interactions
Face to face discussions including at networking events
Letters or flyers sent through the post
Text message marketing
The prospect clicking on your website that has appeared in Google search results

The next time you receive an inquiry, consider what your follow-up process is, and make sure you are using various methods to reach out to your potential customer.

If you meet a potential buyer at a business show, for example, you might want to collect their business card and follow up by connecting with them on LinkedIn, as well as dropping them an email to say it was great meeting them.

Maybe asking them in the email, or in a follow-up phone call, if they would like to meet up to discuss further their interest in your service.

Not having a process to stay in contact can mean lost sales. Without a process, it is easy to forget to take action.

When you know too much…

Before you have a call or a meeting with a prospect, it always helps to do a bit of research first.

An accountant or business coach that understands what the potential client does, what they offer, and other bits of detail is likely to build trust and familiarity quicker.

Afterall, as a business owner, you are more likely to use an accountant or coach that understands your business.

But can it be counter-effective to know too much? Is there a possibility you scare them off by showing how much you know about them?

Actually, it's not the fact that you know too much that can be a problem, it's more about what you share with your client that you know! Let's not split hairs on this. Here's an interesting story that highlights the power of understanding your customer, and it might seem a little bit scary when it comes to the topic of privacy…

In 2012, multiple online sources published articles about how the US retailer Target had identified that a teenage schoolgirl was pregnant, before her father was aware.

The retailer analyzes sales and uses buyer behaviour so that it can tailor its offers to individuals, and, when a teenage girl received coupons for baby clothes and cribs, her father complained.

According to Forbes[11]:

"An angry man went into a Target outside of Minneapolis, demanding to talk to a manager:

"My daughter got this in the mail!" he said. "She's still in high school, and you're sending her coupons for baby clothes and cribs? Are you trying to encourage her to get pregnant?"

The manager didn't have any idea what the man was talking about. He looked at the mailer. Sure enough, it was addressed to the man's daughter and contained advertisements for maternity clothing, nursery furniture and pictures of smiling infants. The manager apologized and then called a few days later to apologize again.

On the phone, though, the father was somewhat abashed. "I had a talk with my daughter," he said. "It turns out there's been some activities in my house I haven't been completely aware of. She's due in August. I owe you an apology."

You might have heard the phrase "big data" or "the power of big data" and this shows how data can be used in marketing to generate more sales.

If used correctly, big data can allow customers to tailor their message to individuals with content that's highly relevant to them. And it can help dramatically increase sales.

---

[11] https://www.forbes.com/sites/kashmirhill/2012/02/16/how-target-figured-out-a-teen-girl-was-pregnant-before-her-father-did/?sh=3dc9e2366668

The issue, however, with the above example is how you can freak out a potential customer if you don't use what you know properly.

When you meet up with a potential client, you might want to say things such as "And I see you have recently launched a new range of products?" or "I saw your latest LinkedIn company update about celebrating 25 years of being in business. Congratulations!".

These kinds of statements are high level and show that you are taking an interest. They don't give a feeling that you are stalking them. Digging deeper however, risks scaring them off, so it's important to know where to draw the line (and getting personal is certainly an area to be cautious with).

Interestingly, Target has changed its campaigns to address this concern. Andrew Pole, who worked at Target commented[12]:

"Then we started mixing in all these ads for things we knew pregnant women would never buy, so the baby ads looked random. We'd put an ad for a lawn mower next to diapers. We'd put a coupon for wineglasses next to infant clothes. That way, it looked like all the products were chosen by chance.

"And we found out that as long as a pregnant woman thinks she hasn't been spied on, she'll use the coupons. She just assumes that everyone else on her block got the same

---

[12] https://www.forbes.com/sites/kashmirhill/2012/02/16/how-target-figured-out-a-teen-girl-was-pregnant-before-her-father-did/?sh=3dc9e2366668

mailer for diapers and cribs. As long as we don't spook her, it works."

Using feedback to increase results

There is an alternative way to build trust with potential and existing customers that's possibly more engaging and less scary.

Asking for feedback from customers is a great way to show that you care - and besides being a great way to understand how to improve your products and services - it also has an even greater impact on customer service when their comments and feedback are implemented.

There are, however, other benefits related to generating new business and long-term clients.

Asking for justification

According to the book, '*Yes! 50 Scientifically Proven Ways to Be Persuasive*', asking people to explain or justify why they have made a decision will lead to a higher commitment to making the decision in the first place.

In other words, someone who has made a decision is less likely to cancel or unsubscribe if they have verbally given a justification to someone for their actions.

The actual reason given doesn't matter. What counts is that the person asked has put in the mental effort to justify their decision, and as a result is more committed to it. This can have a positive and a negative impact.

On the positive side, if a customer justifies why they have signed up to your monthly subscription services, they are more likely to stay with you for longer.

On the other hand, if you find out that a potential customer has decided to buy elsewhere, and you ask why - their justification could well be the nail in the coffin for your sales pitch!

The same principle applies if a customer calls up to cancel.

While it's good to get feedback, it might be best to focus on what you can do to build trust and highlight the benefits of your service, rather than ask why they prefer buying from someone else.

Asking for feedback or asking for a justification can also be worded differently to get a different result.

A restaurant, for example, stopped telling customers "Please call to cancel your reservation" and instead decided to ask, "Will you call and let us know if you need to cancel?"

The result? The number of people who had made reservations but didn't turn up dropped from 30% to 10%!

Let's just look at that figure for a second. If your business takes 100 reservations a week and the number of no-shows drops from 30 to 10, then that's an extra 20 customers.

With an average selling price of $50, that's an extra $1,000 a week in sales ($52,000 a year) just by changing the wording related to your cancellation policy!

You might argue that it's not 20 extra customers. It's 20 customers that aren't lost. However you perceive it, the simple change of wording is easy to implement, and the net result is immense.

Getting it written down

I have heard various business coaches explain over the years how writing down your goals means you are more likely to act on them.

According to Inc.com[13], you are 42% more likely to achieve your goals if you write them down.

I've seen other statistics based on various forms of research, but whatever the figure, there is evidence that writing things down means things are more likely to get done.

So, what does this have to do with customer behavior and growing sales (besides setting goals to achieve this)?

If you want a potential customer to turn up to a follow-up meeting, or if you want a customer who attends your training course to come along to any follow-on courses then get them to write it down!

Research[14] also shows how this worked when asking people to volunteer. Two groups were asked if they could volunteer on an AIDS awareness program at schools.

---

[13] See the article at https://www.inc.com/peter-economy/this-is-way-you-need-to-write-down-your-goals-for-faster-success.html
[14] In the book Yes! 50 Scientifically Proven Ways to Be Persuasive

Of those asked verbally, 17% showed up, but 49% of those asked to fill out a very quick form showed up to help out.

Almost 3 times more people who made a written commitment took the required action.

A change of circumstances

As we have seen, it's very difficult to get someone to change their mind, especially if you have asked them to justify their decision, but there is a way to change this.

As humans, we don't want to show weakness or indecisiveness, so we fear that changing our mind might not reflect well in the eyes of other people.

That's possibly why so many politicians refuse to accept they made a wrong decision. The thought of the media pointing out that they have made a U-turn on their policy might well prevent them from doing the right thing.

If the circumstances change, however, then politicians and customers have a legitimate reason to change their mind - or at least, they perceive it's a legitimate reason!

If a customer has an older model of your product, then they are more likely to upgrade if they understand that the older solution was great at the time, but circumstances have changed a lot since then and newer versions offer more or better functionality.

Highlighting the change in circumstances makes the decision process to switch to your products, or to upgrade to something better that you sell, much easier and more likely.

I recently had a discussion with an agency that offered 'reputation management' as an option when selling its 'post on social media' service. This involved online monitoring of their clients brand on social media and other channels, to help protect the customer from negative comments or any attempts to damage their brand by competitors, disgruntled ex-employees and anyone else who might try to cause issues for them online.

The customer decided not to take the 'reputation management' option, and just used the usual services that they offer. That seemed fair at the time. Many businesses are active on social media and very few have invested in some form of reputation management from a third-party.

Unfortunately, a disgruntled customer of theirs decided to attack the brand on social media, with a continual stream of negative comments that potential new customers could see.

Needless to say, the company decided that with the change in circumstances, it was now time to take the extra service!

The change in circumstances doesn't have to be as extreme as this, and it will depend on your business and the situation with your customer.

It might also be that circumstances have changed, but your customer doesn't realize it - whether that's a change in the law, the weather, advances in technology or the fact that you have introduced a service that you didn't offer before.

When it comes to making a purchasing decision, many people decide not to buy a product or service because it's not right for them at the time.

That doesn't mean your product or service will never be bought. When a customer says no to buying, that should be translated as, 'no, not now at this current moment in time.'.

If circumstances change, then you have a great reason to highlight why a potential customer might change their decision and buy what you have to offer.

Social Proof: Count me in!

According to Wikipedia[15]:

"Social proof is a psychological and social phenomenon wherein people copy the actions of others in an attempt to undertake behavior in a given situation."

Put into simple terms, if a product or service has reviews, recommendations and other people buying it, then there's proof that it's worthy of buying.

The more popular it is, the more socially acceptable it is – and the more people will want to buy it.

Social proof is a powerful concept.

If nobody is buying a product or service, then we tend to think there is something wrong with it, or that we are likely to have a bad experience.

---

[15] https://en.wikipedia.org/wiki/Social_proof

A product or service with a large number of customer reviews, or where people are queuing up to buy, however, can be very enticing.

The human brain is geared to believe that safety comes in numbers, and we are compelled to conform with the characteristics or rules of a group.

When buying something, it doesn't guarantee that the service will be outstanding, or better than a service with lower social proof, but it does reduce the risk of it being a poor experience.

I remember after setting up my business in 2011 being asked at networking events how many customers I have by local businesses who were interested in my services.

It's a tricky situation because as a start-up, you have very few (if any at all!) customers.

You don't want to (and shouldn't) lie, but you know that saying you don't have any customers can be a reason for not getting the sale.

You are at risk of being stuck in a loop where people don't buy because you don't have the social proof, but you won't get the social proof until people buy.

Honesty is always the best policy, and you can put a positive spin on the situation by pointing out how much extra attention they will get as a new customer, or maybe that they are getting a better deal (or launch deal) while you build up your business.

Other options include pointing out why you are unique or highlighting that there's been a terrific response so far from interested buyers, so you expect to be busy with lots of new happy customers soon.

In my corporate days, a competitor for the business I worked for used to sell at cost, or below cost price for the first few orders, effectively buying their first few customers and building up social proof so that they could highlight these big customers in their marketing.

Whatever your strategy for starting up a business, these are only short-term measures. The long-term plan should be to build social proof and make your brand, and what you offer, much more appealing.

Social proof can come in many forms, such as showing how long you have been established, or that you are a down-to-earth caring business through social media, or by demonstrating testimonials and reviews on your website.

Providing social proof can take a customer's final decision from, 'I'm not sure enough if I want to buy', to, 'ok, let's do this. I will make the purchase'.

The type of social proof you use in your marketing can vary depending, firstly, on what social proof you already have, and secondly, on what you believe is more likely to convert visitors for your particular offering or industry.

Here are some examples of social proof you can use in your marketing communications:

Membership: Over 1,000 people have joined our community already!

Purchasing: A customer testimonial such as "Love the product and quality. A must-have for anyone!"

Booking a restaurant: Over 200 people have rated us 5 stars!

Booking a hotel: We have won the TripAdvisor and Late Rooms award for best quality service in 2019!

Serving happy customers for over 25 years!

Even if you have been established for many years, you might not have that many reviews or testimonials.

Customers often need to be prompted to leave a review, so make sure to add this to your process when interacting with customers.

Social Proof in reverse

Social proof is great for getting people to take action, but what about stopping them doing something?

Over the years, I have seen various signs or marketing messages asking people not to do things - but their message also points out how lots of other people also do what they should not.

Examples include asking people not to damage or litter the forest, not to leave things behind, or not to take things that don't belong to them.

Surely telling customers how many other people don't follow the rules is an endorsement and social proof to carry on breaking the rules, right?

In his book 'Yes! 50 secrets from the science of persuasion', Noah Goldstein gives an example of a petrified forest where people were taking the petrified wood home with them.

Putting up a sign at the entrance saying how many people were stealing wood (even though it was an estimated 2% of the visitors) meant that the amount being stolen actually rose dramatically, as it sent a message that it's ok to take the petrified wood if other people are doing it!

Further research showed that changing the sign to show how many people were being good citizens had a positive impact with less wood being taken.

The IRS (or Inland Revenue Service in the US) made a similar mistake by pointing out how many people were evading taxes, making it more acceptable. That was a costly mistake!

You can bear this in mind for your business.

If you are a hotel owner, for example, asking guests to reuse towels, rather than wash them every day, then point out how many people reuse towels rather than how many don't! I know this might not be marketing, per se, but it's worth considering in any messages you send out to your customers.

Start small and use 'priming'

Two more ways that you can build trust with potential customers is by starting small or by priming the customer for the sale, but before we go through what these are, let's dig a little bit deeper into how high (or low) the level of trust must be before a customer makes a purchase.

As a general rule, the more expensive or the more personal the service, the higher the trust level must be.

If you are buying a fizzy drink for pennies, you don't need to build up as much trust with the brand than if you are buying a car or a diamond necklace that will cost you thousands of pounds or dollars.

Similarly, if you're a personal fitness trainer or business consultant, the customer needs to trust that you have the experience to make them, or their business fitter and in better shape, and you wouldn't want to work personally with someone that you don't trust or can't get along with.

Note: I'm not defining exactly how much a customer must spend or how personalized the support must be here. Every business and every customer is different. If the transaction is considered an impulse purchase (i.e., The customer doesn't have to think long and hard before spending any money) then it safe to say that the need to build trust is lower. The longer the customer takes to think about a purchase and the more thought that they put into it, the higher the level of trust typically needs to be.

I am using the word 'typically' as it can vary for every person, business and solution. Just because someone took forever to feel they trusted the brand enough to make a purchase doesn't mean all potential customers will be like that. You might have a customer who took several months while another made a very quick decision.

If your business offers items that are higher priced or require a high level of personal support, then you can jump start the process of building trust by starting small and by priming the customer for the purchase.

What do I mean by a starting small?

Starting small is about having an introductory product or offer that allows the customer to try out your brand. It reduces the barriers to selling by lowering the level of trust needed and by prompting the potential customer to say "heck, why not give it a try to see what it's like".

Another benefit of starting small (that's often overlooked) is that it makes the product more acceptable, and it gets the customer used to using the product or service.

This comes down to having trust in the product or service and building familiarity. A baker can offer small samples of their produce and a software company can provide a cut down version of its software with limited features.

Starting small is a proven way to build familiarity and acceptance and is backed by proven marketing campaigns over time, including my own marketing activities for myself and a growing number of customers.

In one piece of research[16], only 17% of homeowners near a school agreed to have a large "Drive Carefully" sign installed on their front lawn, compared to 76% who agreed in another area. The large difference in the results was down to one thing... starting small.

In the second group, the homeowners were first asked to have a small sign erected. Two weeks later, they were then asked if the small sign could be replaced by the larger one.

Because the homeowners in the second group had become familiar with having the sign in their garden, a much bigger 76% of those originally asked to have a small sign put up had agreed to now have it replaced by a larger sign.

Priming your customers

Priming is similar, and in many cases, you might consider it the same as starting small.

Priming is about preparing the customer for the purchase by setting out the environment in a way that makes saying yes more desirable.

Magicians are experts in priming. They use subtle hand gestures and language so that you are more likely to think of a certain number or card. As one source states[17]:

-

---

[16] https://fs.blog/yes-50-scientifically-proven-ways-to-be-persuasive/

[17] https://www.gold.ac.uk/news/magicians-mind-control-tricks-/#:~:text=Mental%20priming%20force%20%2D%20a%20magicia n,example%2C%20the%20three%20of%20diamonds.

Mental priming force – a magician uses subtle verbal and nonverbal primes to prime the spectator to name a target object. Created by Derren Brown, this technique relies on using subtle hand gestures and key words to prime people to think of, for example, the three of diamonds. This force has been shown to be effective for 18% of participants, when it would be expected less than 2% by chance.

In terms of marketing, we aren't using any tricks. Instead, the focus is more on doing things to build trust and to create acceptance that the product or solution is a good choice.

In the previous research example, a small sign was used to prime the customer so that they were more likely to accept the larger one.

Here are some examples of how priming can be used to help a customer with their decision-making process:

Similar to the roadkill café story in Chapter 3, a restaurant can play Italian music to prime their customers and help sell more Italian wine.

An accountant can write a blog or email about the risks of trying to avoid paying tax before contacting clients about their auditing services or insurance (assuming their customer has read the email or blog first).

A health-related company can provide fun wordsearches for its clients that include healthy words related to healthy food and getting exercise.

Your business can create a brand logo and strapline that primes your target audience for what you offer. Nike does this with their "Just Do It" slogan.

If you aren't convinced that a blog, email campaign or wordsearch will impact how we think and react, consider this:

In 1996, John Bargh, a psychologist at Yale published research[18] showing how specific words related to old age caused people to walk slower!

Two groups were asked to create sentences out of a range of given words. Both groups were told that the words were random, but one of the groups was actually given words related to old age, such as "wrinkle", "alone" and "bingo".

Once the exercise was complete, they were secretly timed to see how long it took them to walk down the corridor to the exit.

The group that was given the age-related words, on average, walked much more slowly.

How does this impact your business, and what does it have to do with building trust?

Using the right words and priming your potential customer helps to build familiarity with you and the services that you provide.

---

[18] https://mindsetforsuccess.com.au/phenomenal-energy-of-words/

What you offer might be unfamiliar and scary to them – and if you jump in at the deep end with your sales pitch then they are more likely build up that fear.

By using priming, the customer slowly builds up that confidence and trust so that they are more likely to buy from you when the time is right.

Action!

Spend 20 minutes now reviewing how you position your product or service to your customers and ask yourself "How can I improve the initial interactions with the customer to build trust?"

If you have potential customers who aren't committing to buy from you then start small and offer them a trial or a limited version of your solution. Once they start using your solution, they will most likely want to keep on using it.

Earlier (in the chapter about pricing), we talked about the power of free to generate more sales and this is very similar in principle. You might want to play around with different options and test out what works best. Do you get better results offering something for free, or by starting small?

If the sales process requires educating the customer of the benefits of what you do and how your offering works, then focus on priming.

Fun fact!

Did you know that the happier you are and the better your mood, the more likely you are to spend more money?

This is nothing new to retail where food stores put vibrant looking healthy fruit and veg as the first thing you see when entering the store[1920]. Another example of priming being used in marketing!

---

[20] https://theconversation.com/the-science-that-makes-us-spend-more-in-supermarkets-and-feel-good-while-we-do-it-23857

Chapter 7: The impact of color, words and choice

Many of us have an understanding that the appearance of marketing materials and wording we use can impact sales.

We appreciate that a professional appearance and wording is needed if we want someone to buy what's on offer, but our knowledge is only on a superficial or simple level.

We have a sense or gut feeling that the wording or formatting isn't great, but we often don't understand how different wording or colors are impacting the way a customer reacts.

An advert, for example, that is badly written, or has swearing, will put people off, while a professional advert with a great-looking font, and great colors is attractive, but if we dig into the detail of the advert, there are some changes that can make people want to buy or that can urge them to take action.

In this chapter, we discuss how colors such as blue, yellow, and orange can impact the way we react as well as wording and fonts.

This includes words called 'Power Words', which are proven to increase conversion rates when used in marketing materials.

We will also talk about how many choices or options you should give customers, and whether it's best to offer a range of product or service options, or to keep the options limited.

How color impacts your purchase habits

The colors you use in marketing should always be in line with your overall branding for your business, but there's a little secret that not many people know – certain colors impact the way people think and the decisions they make!

According to Kissmetrics, in their blog post[21], red "increases heart rate" and "creates urgency".

Red is ideal as a call to action in discounted or clearance sales, while orange is "aggressive" and "creates a call to action" such as "subscribe, buy or sell".

Both red and orange are recommended for call-to-action buttons, but if you want to increase trust in your marketing, consider blue.

If you sell luxury products, consider black as the main theme. Black also conveys professionalism while pink and purple are more effective with fashion and beauty products.

Here is a breakdown of the various colors, and how they impact the way we think about a brand:

Purple with its blend of red and blue evokes mystery, sophistication, spirituality and royalty. Lavender evokes nostalgia and sentimentality.

---

[21] https://blog.kissmetrics.com/color-psychology/

Gold provokes feelings of wealth and success. It suggests opulence and is perfect for high-end items such as jewelry, or when targeting wealthy people. It gives an allure of status and charisma.

White is clarity and simplicity. It also shows a brand being clean and clutter-free.

The human eye sees white as being bright, so it's highly effective at catching someone's attention. If used with a small number of objects on a page or advert, then the eye is drawn to those objects more easily.

This is highly effective when having a call to action or a button that you want people to interact with. White is also often used with health and well-being products.

Gray evokes calm neutral feelings. Although this color is often considered 'boring', used properly it can reflect a certain maturity in a brand as well as authority and stability.

Black is sophisticated, professional, formal and luxurious. It works well for professional or expensive products, but it can ruin the image of a brand if used too much in some areas such as a website that is completely black.

Green suggests health, freshness and serenity, and is also used to reflect the environment and being environmentally friendly.

Green's meaning varies with its many shades. While deeper greens are associated with wealth or prestige, light greens are considered to be calming.

Brown is popular with organic and natural food and beauty products. It's simple, strong, durable and honest.

Blue is trustworthy, suggests stability and is universally well-liked. It can be highly effective when used with white and small amounts of black.

While yellow can infer cheapness in products, it's also associated with the sun and conveys a happy or positive brand.

Yellow communicates optimism, positivity and warmth. If you want your messaging to stand out, or you want to convey being price competitive, then yellow can be effective in doing that.

Pink is great for fashion and beauty products and conveys youthfulness and romance. It can, however, infer a lower price if you are selling beauty products compared to using colors such as black and green.

We have already discussed red, which activates your pituitary gland, increases heart rate
and causes you to breathe more rapidly. This response makes red great for grabbing people's attention and creating urgency.

Which colors will you go for?

The colors you use depend on the messaging, and what you want to achieve. What you use on packaging and your product could be different compared to what you use on a website landing page where you want visitors to take action.

At the very least, ensure to use color and styling in line with your branding, and I strongly consider using orange or red for your call to action!

Power Words for Greater Sales

So many people under-appreciate the power of using the right words, and with a few changes to their wording, they could get much better results from marketing campaigns (including websites, social media posts, email marketing and so on).

According to Buffer in their blog article '189 Powerful Words That Convert'[22], power words are so important that in a marketing campaign that "one word can change everything". I completely agree.

We rarely consider how important certain words can be in influencing how we perceive something, or the decision we make. Adding one single power word could increase conversions on a website by as much as 20%.

Power words, as the name suggests, are words that hold power. They are words that make the difference when making a statement.

Would you be more inclined to take action if someone tells you their services will *guarantee* results, rather than just tell you they will get results?

---

[22] blog.bufferapp.com/words-and-phrases-that-convert-ultimate-list

Would you rather I helped you to create a marketing campaign or to create a *successful* marketing campaign?

The word 'successful' is suggestive and makes the offer more desirable while the word 'guarantee' reduces the risk of buying the services and increases the confidence in what is being bought.

Sometimes a power word can be a simple adjective (or word that describes something) that's positive in nature. A restaurant may offer *delicious* ice cream, while a team building events company may offer 5 *proven* ways to motivate team members.

Many power words are not descriptive but can be even more powerful than many of the others. The word 'now' and 'hurry' are examples.

During our childhood, we are trained to do things 'now'. Screaming parents to the tune of 'put your shoes on now', 'we are running late, eat your food now' and, 'for the fifth time, brush your teeth now!' may be great examples that some of us may remember well!

Upon reading the word 'now', many visitors are prompted at a subconscious level to take action.

Who would have thought that the three letters n, o and w could be so powerful!

Similarly, the word 'hurry' as in the sentence, 'hurry, this offer won't last!' is claimed to prompt the reader to take action. It tells the user's brain at a subconscious level to hurry into action and click on the buy button. Although the word hurry is effective, I don't believe it's quite as effective as the word 'now' which invokes a much stronger response.

Here are some power words worth considering in your marketing:

Achieve – Amazing – Authentic – Avoid
Best-Selling – Easily – Exclusive – Free
Guarantee – Guaranteed– Hurry – Improved
Instantly – Jaw-dropping – Limited - No-Risk – Now
Offer – Only – Priceless – Quick – Proven
Remarkable – Results – Safe – Secret
Successful – Tested – You – Unique - Value

When writing copy for your marketing, make sure to use power words. Obviously, don't go overboard by sticking power words everywhere. It's important to find the right balance and keep the content easy to read - and for the message to be clearly understood.

Visitors may be put off by your 'incredible, unique, amazing, limited time offer for your proven product that you must take advantage of now and that's exclusive and only available to you…'. Yawn.

The power of three

When it comes to effective marketing messaging, you can also get great results by using the power of three.

Have you ever asked someone what they do and ended up feeling confused and bamboozled by their somewhat complex response? If only they were clearer on what they, or their business does – or what the benefits are.

Enter, the power of three.

Believe it or not, us humans have a great memory (apart from when trying to find the car keys).

The problem is that we have too much to remember, and there are too many distractions trying to prevent us from remembering certain things.

So, to remember things, we tend to find it easier to remember things in groups of three.

If I give you a list of 9 or 10 numbers, you might find it hard to remember but, if you break it down into sets of 3 then it's easier.

For example:

213674245 is hard to remember, but if we break it down:
213-674-245 is much easier.

From Martin Luther King Jr. and Julius Caesar to Winston Churchill and the American Declaration of Independence, the power of three has been used effectively over the years to make the message clear:

"I came, I saw, I conquered" (Julius Caesar)
"Blood, sweat and tears" (Winston Churchill)
"Life, Liberty and the pursuit of happiness". (American Declaration of Independence)
"Insult, injustice and exploitation" (Martin Luther King Jr)

These are great, highly effective and memorable ways to get the message across. If Martin Luther King had mentioned 6 or 7 things, then it would have been harder to remember, and the message would have become diluted.

In your marketing communication you can also use the power of 3 as follows (and yes, there are 3 ways listed!):

- Make your product memorable for when people are ready to buy
- To get the benefits across quickly and easily without losing the attention of your audience
- To show how easy to use your product is, resulting in higher trust and consequent sales

Here are some examples to consider:

An accountant might highlight they offer ways to *save on tax, avoid fines and grow your business* as the main benefits.

A web designer might increase the value of a service by offering a 3 in 1 package: web design, blogging and social media for one single price.

A software company might communicate that their product can be set up in 3, easy to follow steps.

A fashion designer might use a slogan such as 'look great, feel amazing, be different'

Whether you use 3 or another number in your marketing, it's important to keep messages simple and easy to understand. The right words are important, and I recommend using the power of three in your messaging to increase the chances of success.

Fonts

Similar to color, it's important to make sure that the fonts you use in your marketing are consistent. It's recommended to use a maximum of 2 or 3 different fonts across all of your marketing materials.

All headlines or titles can be in one font, while the main body of the content on your website and in marketing brochures can be in another font.

Having too many fonts looks untidy, reduces trust with the reader, and puts them off making a purchasing decision. Consistency, however, increases trust.

So, which fonts should you use?

There are hundreds of different fonts available that you can use so picking one can be a challenge. Many are free, and there are quite a lot that you can buy for a small fee.

When it comes to selecting a font, there's no hard and fast rule as to which is best, but I recommend selecting one with the style that fits your business.

If your business is about providing handwritten letters, providing antique products or it's related to health and well-being, then fonts that are more wavy, or that look like handwriting are more acceptable (fonts such as Parisienne, Mark Script or Bad Script).

Brands that sell business to business, however, should use less wavy fonts such as Open Sans.

Another important consideration is how easy the font is to read. Fonts that are hard to read will put off potential customers, and this could result in lost business.

I recommend not using Times New Roman. Although this font is very popular, it's also very hard to read, and can have a negative impact on potential customers.

How too much choice leads to poor sales results

Over the years, we have got used to an increasing range of options when buying - from different car brands and car types to places to shop for everyday consumables such as mobiles, stationery or home and kitchenware.

You only have to walk down the aisle of your local supermarket to see how many cereals, sauces or wines and beers are available.

We have been programmed over the years to believe that a wide range of choice is good.

Why settle for a small coupe in a color you don't like, when you can have a spacious SUV in the color you like - and with optional extras you love?

Ask any consumer if they would like as much choice as possible and the answer will pretty much always be YES.

Unfortunately, too much choice for your customers can harm sales. Consider this:

In 2010, the Economist magazine[23] reported on research where jams were available to taste as samples outside a store, and a coupon was offered to consumers to redeem on a jam they liked in the store opposite.

When a choice of 24 jams was offered, 3% of consumers made a purchase, but when the number of samples was reduced to only 6 options, the conversion rate (or the number of people who went on to make a purchase) increased from 3% to an incredible 30%.

It seems like less choice made the decision to purchase much easier.

This research has been backed up over the years by various articles such as *Why Too Much Choice Is Stressing Us Out by the Guardian*[24] and books such as *The Paradox of Choice: Why More Is Less* by Barry Schwartz.

It seems that although we like the idea of choice, it's not always a good thing. So, what has this got to do with marketing?

When designing your solutions, it's important to keep it simple. Having too many choices can increase the chances of a consumer not buying.

---

[23] Source: http://www.economist.com/node/17723028

[24] Source: https://www.theguardian.com/lifeandstyle/2015/oct/21/choice-stressing-us-out-dating-partners-monopolies

Limiting the options makes it easier for the customer to make a decision and to buy from you.

When sending a quote or proposal to a customer, it's best to limit the options and make it clear that you are flexible.

Rather than listing 7 or 8 ways to go forward, provide 1 or 2 along with wording that makes it clear that you are happy to discuss other options.

You should have identified what your customer wants from talking to them before sending the proposal, so a lot of options aren't needed.

Limiting the options in a proposal reduces the risk of them not making a decision because they can't decide. It also looks more professional. If you provide too many options, it sends the message that you don't know what's right for the customer.

Earlier, we discussed Decoy Pricing which involves 3 options. This is ok when providing a pricing table or price list but I wouldn't provide any more options than that, unless you feel it's absolutely necessary.

Chapter 8: The power of story telling

Everybody loves a story, don't they? For the purposes of this book and generating more sales, we aren't talking about the type of story you tell the kids at bedtime (or that you used to get read to you).

We are talking about painting a visual picture, or story that your target audience can relate to.

In marketing, there has been a focus to tell a story about a brand, whether that's to paint a picture of how or why they need what that brand offers, or to help customers to understand the brand and the business.

A story can, for example, highlight the mission and values of a company that they want their customers to buy into, or it can be a way of introducing the team and the work that they do.

So, why does storytelling work?

People remember things and are more likely to buy when they see a brand or brand message telling a story.

A charity gets more responses when pointing out that 8-year-old Joel is going without food or water, than if it says that hundreds or thousands of people are dying of malnutrition and lack of drinking water.

The reason that this stands out is because we can associate with poor Joel, and the situation he is in. We can relate to him as a human and become compassionate about the situation, whereas we can't do that with a statistic such as hundreds or thousands of people.

The human mind finds it easier to associate with the story of an individual or a single brand than a large number or any other form of statistic.

I don't want to get into ethics or politics here, but Joseph Stalin, unfortunately, was once quoted as saying '*A Single Death is a Tragedy; a Million Deaths is a Statistic*'. He meant it from a different perspective, but the quote highlights how many of us perceive - and the media often report the news.

In his book, '*The Black Swan*', Nicolas Taleb refers to this as the 'Narrative Fallacy'. The fact that we believe a situation is the way it is because of the story that has been painted - regardless of if it's true or not.

This is a negative way of looking at it, but the fact remains, that if you create a good story about your brand, you are more likely to grow your business and get sales.

Using wine to tell a story

Seth Godin in one of his books[25] describes how wine experts effectively convince themselves that wine tastes much better when served in Riedel wine glasses, when it fact, it doesn't.

How can trusted and experienced wine experts get it wrong?

---

[25] For more information read 'All Marketers Are Liars' by Seth Godin

How can they be convinced that the wine tastes better, despite evidence showing that the wine does not change in any way, shape or form when using these wine glasses?

They believe that the wine is better, Seth argues, because the experts have created their own story about how the wine tastes, and this has caused them to truly believe that the wine glasses make a difference.

The story that has been created, either by the makers of the wine glasses, or by the experts themselves in their own minds, has overpowered any other signals such as smell and taste that's telling them that the wine is no different.

Seth Godin also argues that businesses don't tell or create a story - the customer does. The business talks about its brand and the customer creates the story themselves from that. This seems to be support by Taleb in his book when he refers to the narrative fallacy.

This argument is understandable, but I'm not going to get into the debate over whether it's the brand or the customer that creates the story.

Businesses can either create a great story for customers to buy into, or they can set the scene, and 'nudge' the customer to create their own story of the brand in a positive way.

Either way, there are plenty of things you can do as part of the story creation process for your customers...

Ways to tell a story

There are various ways you can build a story around your brand. Making it personal with stories behind how the business came to be who it is, and what the mission is, can be highly effective.

For example, a local sports club can talk about how it is on a mission to improve the health and lives of local people and bring the community together.

It could be that the company was set up after the owner (let's call him John since having a name builds on the story) had a change in his personal circumstances.

Potential customers or people in the community can relate to this story and will want to 'buy in' to the mission and the brand.

A personal coach can create a story around how they want to change the lives of people, and demonstrate how he or she has a daily routine that inspires people to want to join in.

And a software company can highlight the friendly team of developers, and support people in their business, dedicated to helping small businesses do their jobs better, quicker and with less hassle.

These are just a few examples of how you can build a story that makes your company more memorable, and that helps customers want to buy from you.

It's important that the stories you tell are ethical and genuine.

For further examples of how famous people and brands have successfully built up their brand around a positive story, think of Richard Branson at Virgin or James Dyson who tells a great story around how persistence and perseverance led to him inventing the bagless vacuum cleaner.

Summary & Resources

There are lots of ways that you can create products and services, and many ways you can position or communicate pricing and your marketing messaging to attract more customers and grow your sales.

We have covered many of the major ways you can do these in this book.

The aim of this book is to give you ideas to help your business that you can use ethically in your sales and marketing. When it comes to being ethical, don't, for example, make claims about what you offer that aren't true.

Marketing is often more than just about sending out a few emails and tweets, and I hope this book has highlighted how important perception is, based on various factors from the wording you use, to the number and type of products and services you offer.

The next time you put together a marketing campaign, or you are involved in a sales-related activity, ask yourself the following:

- Am I using the right words, and colors?
- Am I keeping the messaging and choices simple?
- How am I building trust and social proof with potential buyers?
- How can I do things better and get better results, based on what I have read in this book?

Start with the brand and the essence of your business

We've seen how pricing, perception, colors and product design work together to influence customers – and these factors (among others that we have discussed) shouldn't be treated in separate silos.

The optimum approach is to start with what your brand and your business is about, and then work on design, messaging and other things after.

There's no point, for example, designing a brand that says "we're cheap" with a product that's high-quality and very expensive.

Decide what your brand is about – your values, your mission and your identity. Create a logo and business approach that fits with that and then focus on designing a product and pricing it in line with your brand. Consistency is key.

A BIG Thanks!

Many thanks for taking the time to read Psychology in Marketing and Sales. I really appreciate that you have chosen to read a book that I have spent many hours writing.

Although it's a relatively small book, it has still taken a lot of time and effort to build the structure and research data to back up what I have written about, so a big, big thanks!

If you have any questions, feel free to email me at Darren@thinktwicemarketing.com.

I also have a list of power words that you can use in your marketing so email me if you would like a copy (make sure to mention that you are looking for the power words guide).

You may also want to check out my marketing blogs using the URL below:

www.thinktwicemarketing.com/blog

If you have enjoyed this book, please do leave a review on Amazon.

It would really be appreciated and most importantly, your review will help others who might find the book of value.

We have covered a lot in this book, but we aren't quite finished yet!

At the back of the book is a list of books and websites which provide further information.

Some of the materials listed have been an inspiration to me in writing this book, and I hope they will inspire you as well.

Many thanks again, and I wish you all the best in your marketing efforts!

~ Darren

Resources to help you

Books

Here is a list of books that inspired me when writing this book:

Freakonomics: A Rogue Economist Explores the Hidden Side of Everything by Steven D. Levitt

Yes!: 50 Scientifically Proven Ways to Be Persuasive by Noah Goldstein

All Marketers Are Liars by Seth Godin

Tribes by Seth Godin

Predictably Irrational by Dan Ariely

Hooked: How to Build Habit-Forming Products by Nir Ayal

Made to Stick: Why some ideas take hold and others come unstuck by Chip and Dan Heath

Thinking, Fast and Slow by Daniel Kahneman

The Black Swan by Nicolas Taleb

All of these books provide great insights into how the human mind works when making decisions such as what to buy. Some of the books, such as Freakonomics and The Black Swan are not marketing focused but still provide some fascinating insights.

If you would like further help with your marketing, I also discuss marketing techniques to help you with your business in my books 'How to Create a Perfect Landing Page' and 'How to Create a Successful Email Marketing Campaign'. Both of which are available on Amazon.

Websites

The following websites and blog pages have some great information and ideas for improving your sales and marketing when it comes to understanding the human mind. Don't forget to check out my blogs as well. I've included the URL:

https://seths.blog/
(Seth is a well-known marketing expert who writes regular but usually short blog posts)

www.thinktwicemarketing.com/blog

https://www.neurosciencemarketing.com/

https://blog.hubspot.com/marketing/psychology-marketers-revealing-principles-human-behavior

https://buffer.com/resources/marketing-psychology

Printed in Great Britain
by Amazon